Gods of Babel
JUDITH MOK

salmonpoetry

Published in 2011 by
Salmon Poetry
Cliffs of Moher, County Clare, Ireland
Website: www.salmonpoetry.com
Email: info@salmonpoetry.com

Copyright © Judith Mok, 2011

ISBN 978-1-907056-80-2

All rights reserved. No part of this publication may be reproduced or transmitted in any form or by any means, electronic or mechanical, including photography, recording, or any information storage or retrieval system, without permission in writing from the publisher. The book is sold subject to the condition that it shall not, by way of trade or otherwise, be lent, resold or otherwise circulated without the publisher's prior consent in any form of binding or cover other than that in which it is published and without a similar condition, including this condition, being imposed on the subsequent purchaser.

COVER IMAGE: Hans Memling "Two horses in a landscape". Museum Boijmans Van Beuningen, Rotterdam.
COVER DESIGN: *Siobhán Hutson*

PRINTED IN IRELAND

Salmon Poetry receives financial support from The Arts Council

for Cassius and Ezra

Acknowledgements

Thanks are due to the editors of the following where some of these poems appeared: *The Stinging Fly, Poetry Ireland Review, Mediterranean Poetry, The Parlour Review, Landing Places* (Dedalus Press), *Shine On* (Dedalus Press), RTE Radio, and NDR Television.

The author also gratefully acknowledges the following: The Arts Council of Ireland, Culture Ireland, the Cill Railaig Foundation and Marina Guinness.

Contents

Yesterday I was Conceived Again	11
Orfeo and Eurydice	12
Recognising Tenderness	13
Muse	14
November Beach	15
February Fields	16
Get Physical	17
The Gods of Babel	18
Red	19
Oasis	20
The Roots of the Myth is a Monkey Maybe	21
Responsorum Questions and Answers	23
Woke Up	24
Who	25
Hopscotch	27
What the Wind Refuses to Tell Me	28
When I Do Do Don't sleep	29
Solitude Snow White	30
Belle	32
A Rose with a Name	34
Jellyfish	35
Short Poems	36
Amsterdam	37
Amsterdam Sunday	38
Iranian Persian, My Darling	39

Song	40
Chanson	41
Cannot Write Songs	42
Heavy as a Butterfly	43
Heya! Heya! Kesckemet! A Tale Well Told	44
Little Red Riding Hood	45
Blood or "Le Sang des Autres"	46
A Point of View	47
All the Other Answers	48
Walkabout	49
Einstein	51
A Cold Poem	52
Could I Have Shared	53
France	54
Make or Break	55
The Wizard's Walk	56
Hands in Cages Louise Bourgeois	58
Beethoven in New York	59
Skull	62
Baudelaire and the Blue Moonstone	63
Adio Querido	64
Choices Incarnate	65
About the Author	67

He who does not believe in miracles is not a realist
The Talmud

Yesterday I was Conceived Again

Yesterday they met: Colette, extravagant French writer, *écrivain, femme de lettres*, seductress. And Louise Bourgeois, infinitely great sculptor, artist of intense integrity, loyal and depressive, innovative, *pensant a maman toujours maman*. I had the two *Mamans* yesterday, two new people started making love and they conceived: me. In the afternoon they listened to Debussy and had the Faun dancing on their table while they ate and held hands and admired each other's hair. But then, when the wine coloured their lips and the food satisfied their direct appetites, they listened to the great Sopranos, pulmonary women, singing into their lives, tending to their dreams and erotic nervous systems and they made love to each other's minds and the soft skin on their bodies, large and warm, small and dry they conceived: me.

Now I am as green as grass, waving my arms in the air in despair, trying to catch that feeling of *umpff, yes umpffeefee* they gave me.

Yesterday I wore a blanket and I knew that the contrasting image down there, seen from my balcony in the night, was the reflection of my life: light swans on dark water.

Today my new mothers are helping me to develop this – white in black – picture of me. *Merci mes Cheries*....

Orfeo and Eurydice
A misunderstanding

When I was with you
I wanted to disappear up your mouth
Where it was soft and singing
And I could hear you live

So: You danced
Holding your limbs away from me
Just enough to create a third thick body of desire
And: I danced, still dance, poor as a beggar
With my beautiful clothes turned to rags

What is there to say about you
When you make me able
To word my silence

You never told me I had died, Orfeo
I came back as Eurydice with your voice singing
And the killer snake on a leash.

In the dark fields where we once met
I picked a passionflower from my hair
It was tied up: The way you like it.

I breathe until my soul is a cold lung
And my song goes unheard

I am travelling, Ice Queen suddenly
You, Ice King, made me play this:
Game of floats, never: Check

You were never my friend
Never my lover – never my never
And now I only miss: You

Recognising Tenderness

I recognized something in the landscape of Connemara. Its threatening beauty is grabbing your eyes and your heart and in your head you want to run away from it as fast as you can.

I sang and sang for the people and was angry in the morning and the night.

So I sat on a beach and gathered stones while making a mental list of the contras in my life and thinking how I should be sitting there reading Wittgenstein instead of rubbing and admiring the flat grey stone that caught my attention, more than the marbled or pink ones. I listened to the sea and moved into the abandoned house on the island across from me. I had smoke coming out of all its tall chimneys and songs in every room. I was in love with the ghost who lived there with me. He drowned on the way back to the mainland. I was a better swimmer.

That's what's making me angry. And sad.

I fell out of love with the ghost and the house stood dark and devoid of song.

But then

In a cold church where the air caught my voice like a cloud I saw the stained glass windows of Harry Clarke and the roses of Klimt he had borrowed and reportrayed.

I remembered the embrace in a Klimt painting as the utmost expression of tenderness I have ever seen. There: Tenderness reportrayed.

Some people spread it around and it goes unrecognized by them, others capture it in their art making us long for it.

While we face the recreaters of tenderness and sing in the cold air with a hard inner stare on perfection, we crave, we must crave for it.

Muse

Why
Would you want to feed my mouth
With gritty Irish words
With soft seductive smoke
With a tongue tied to your heart

November Beach

Maybe I wished for you my entire life
The way you stood with your hands in your pockets
As if they were filled with gifts
I noticed you first on that November beach
There was nothing to break or tear
Or reach out for in you; you were, suddenly, simply there

February Fields

Finding the February fields,
Our feet hitting clumps of clay.
What we heard flapping in the wind
In the old empty stables stacked with ghost cattle
Was a piece of rusting iron that tuned in with us, our mute singing.
These autumn leaves, gathered like gold,
Did not remind me of the sad spring to come.
Why would I want to quote Verlaine:
"Voici des fruits, des fleurs, des feuilles et des branches"
When walking with you
Is like making love to nature.

Get Physical

Saints are to be celebrated.

This year I started honouring the holy ones in a very physical manner.

First in India where I ran around a bonfire in the streets with an Indian poet and his entire family celebrating a Goddess by throwing popcorn on the fire, to feed her, and then perform mad dances to make her come alive.

I climbed the mountains of Bhutan, never losing sight of Mount Everest, to visit the Buddhas and gods of Bhutan and bow to their golden glow at the expense of my heavy lungs, deprived of oxygen, and my legs wanting to wobble away from me after a couple of hours of solid upwards yearning to reach the gods seated in their shrines.

I came back to Ireland to celebrate my own inner beliefs, gods are not involved here, and take a walk on the vast grounds around a friend's house, sharing so much of the recognition of the ground under our feet and the trees and the mountains in our eyes that it felt like my first walk on earth outside time, remembering the past and the future and how your body can take over the pace of your thoughts and leave you lightness to celebrate the god of nature.

Now it was St Patrick who needed an accolade. Already been and gone: the day seen from the top of a Wicklow mountain with so much of the Irish mysticism written in the landscape, the river down in the valley, reflecting its steel in the sun.

In the company of comforting bodies, great minds until late in the night.

Then, the Brazilian drums took over my feet and I danced and danced for Saint Patrick and all......

The Gods of Babel

The gods of Babel went quiet
When I knelt down and begged for a translation
So sure was I that every stain on your mouth
Meant a word with some significance;
These stains were letters written in deep crimson
Emphasized by a bright bloodied background,
An uneven lipped alphabet that was displayed
For my desire to decipher and read:
This is it, this is what I mean – you mean
That I came to believe in the truth of those dark stains
And forgot to turn back towards the light

Red

for Marion Kelly

The world burst out
Of its own maps
And gods changed their names
People talked till Babylon fell
While my heart grew
Into a bitter rose
That bled for you.
I handed you that flower
We did not feast on its perfume together.
It was given to me
By the winged Master of Muses
To celebrate a most terrible union
That is called separation
And is red torment to the
Hundredth power
That is purest and blackest of all

Oasis

I am standing in the desert with my feet in the deep blue water. I can feel the sun on my face and I can remember Messiean *quatuor pour la fin d'un temps* so well that I can see the notes hanging amongst the trees of my "Fata Morgana."

An oasis would be the end of some time, and yet it's hard to decide what type of oasis I want to dwell in.

So, I ride around in circles on my camel's back enjoying the sour-smelling steam that comes off his coat. Jonas, that's his name.

At least I can share the new time I have stepped into with one animal. No I am not going to turn it into an animal farm, this oasis. A six hundred and thirty seat theatre with worldwide broadcast facilities.

Watch it! We are the greatest, Jonas and I.

For the moment. I am all for ornaments on my songlines. Look, I am veiled in indigo wraps, apart from my mouth: a Touareg, a blue, blue rag. Can you hear me?

This has now been broadcast to the millions.

All is quiet in my oasis; I have gone for a swim. My head is bobbing on the surface. My body is caught in the deepest well of water.

I am singing.

The Roots of the Myth is a Monkey Maybe

I had seen it. Sitting there in the middle of a floating island drifting down the brown waters of the Paraná, that long wild river in South America. I was standing on the shores of the Paraná in the city of Paraná in Argentina and I saw the monkey in its reddish brown fur, playing with some roots, undisturbed by the waters that surrounded him. I watched and watched smaller and bigger islands of grass and tiny bushes float down the river and then came the one with the monkey.

Oh, I knew other animals lived on these tiny islands like snakes and rats, but them I did not see.

The monkey was mine. I had been looking at it lying on my bed back in teenage Holland, pleasantly hallucinating about the animal seated on the back of a sturdy horse looking down at the river leaning over towards the other horse that was drinking from the river as well. This was a reproduction of a painting by Memling, a Flemish painter from long ago, and I always wanted to know about the monkey. How did it happen to sit on the back of one of those big horses, horses that are now becoming extinct because we don't use them anymore. Horses like Bruin, Brown on whose broad back I rode so often, bareback, in the woods and on the beaches of my early childhood when I was that little reddish brown monkey. Horses like the ones in the Italian battlefields painted by Uccello, horses that can safely gallop with you into your wildest dreams.

In my bed I listened to Dylan and The Band and to Palestrina and Josquin's church music and the monkey never turned around from the painting to look me in the eye.

Until I saw it again now, this year in India in an old book about myths, in a dark shop. It sat on the horse looking at me with the other white horse beside it. I breathed dust and damp in the shop, drank tea, growing old suddenly while I listened to the man telling me about this monkey of wisdom and how he was part of an Indian myth.

He was also part of my myth; otherwise he wouldn't have turned around for me after so many years.

I saw the monkeys in the city and along the roads and I even sent a picture of one to another continent as a message of wisdom. I had arrived in a place where it was time for me to take over the myth and take the horses to the water.

Responsorum Questions and Answers

In the San Marco cathedral in Venice the monks stood on either side of the church looking down on the gossiping, manipulating, money-making *Bourgeoisie*. They sang Gregorian at first, than the great composers like Monteverdi entered the questions and answering game.

I am drinking Champagne right now, my head is full of bubbles and my ears are beginning to hear the aching intervals of Monteverdi's music in that same head as well. My head, that is.

Meanwhile the monks are clear voiced, young and straight-backed with eyes full of music, chords on small texts they throw at each other like a ballgame and the church amplifies their sound, amplifies the beauty of it. How simple the answers and the questions and the questions and the answers were back then. Or were they? Not really, I should think, but I don't want to think. I am drinking *gesprister*.

The same that I drank back in Vienna with G and H and we sang a Trio outside a pub, interchanging our parts, so out of tune that they threw stale bread at us from the windows of the alleyway where we stood and sang.

No questions and answers there. G is at the Opera now and H, ah H, he is an architect of houses and of his life I suppose. I want to remember the *Lamento della Ninfa*: The woman sighing in a tiny upwards semidemi tone line, *amor, amor* and the three men wailing *miserella*, miserable creature.

Argh, the pleasure of having three brilliantly singing men wailing with you, little unhappy nymph.

But. So: the singing went this way and that way in the church while the Bishop got cold feet and the people colder feet, but the monks didn't stop for hours, they didn't care. They were caught in the web of chords created.

Now I am caught in a silence in between some chords. I build up some questions and I build up some answers. I can't hear the chords though, only minimal music, one, two notes on silence.

Woke up, with a different alphabet in my head.

It finally happened. I can still hear people talk, on the radio, on the canal beneath my window, I can remember that those close to me opened their beautiful lips and sounds came out, apparently meaningful, but I cannot understand anything, because today I spell the world; my world.

The edge is hard and I'm not looking down any abyss beyond it: It might look back at me.

Who
after Brecht

We left him at the Fair
With his girls, Poppy and Corny
Which is short for Cornflower
We knew he liked blue
So Corny was Number One
But Poppy could be wound up
And spread her petals so gracefully
He likes them both, he likes them all
That's why we left him at the Fair
Oh, moon of curious candy floss
Oh, sugar sucking babe
Who will do you, can I do you both?

We, the other guys with girls
Sat in the car and waited for him
To shoot straight at the Fair
Oh, moon of curious candy floss
We watched him walk away
With his hat on his hair
His legs apart, his shoulders square
But for his head, which wasn't really there

Then Poppy came back
And told us he told her that nothing was there
And Corny sucked till she was blue in the face
And sugar was in the moon with the candy floss
When she left him for the next race

Poppy and Cornflower
Died beside our car
Withered with the cold:
Because now it was winter

He'd told them he was the sun
And wanted to shine on them
And juggle four seasons in one,
Spin the mill under the moon of curious candy floss
And hit the whores hard
Who wants who?
Who does red? Who does blue?

Hopscotch

Home: I am there ready to jump. Turn my back on base, where I'm supposed to go. Tonight I want to jump into something I have drawn with an inerasable piece of cray on the borders of an empty, darkened space. And then, I am back in Bergen where I want to go to the dunes and feel the dirty sand grind in between my toes until I reach that open space where I once pushed a classmate out of a tree and then walked all the way home, five miles of talking to the birds and inhaling the sweet, sweet smell of honeysuckle. I walked. Where was my bicycle? Why was I walking? Mother. Home, hopscotch drawn out in front of the house, a brick road, red stones, warm from the afternoon sun, my Siamese cat lying in the middle of the road. No traffic. Mother, laughing and singing in her raw, high voice, French, Russian ballads. Smiling.

Now I understand Ingmar Bergman, you wonderful filmmaker, even better, how he wrote that in the end all he wanted was to hit his bed at home and the tight clean white linen, the soft pillows, the windows open to the wind in the night.

What the Wind Refuses to Tell Me

At night I am covered by a veil and I dream about the same person, a killer, while the hot wind is blowing. So I get up and watch the sun rise over the sea and I go down the wooden stairs, I forget to wear clothes and I swim for a long time in a pool overgrown with lavender until morning comes and I can hum a gentle song and talk to the people who like to have breakfast.

When I Do Do Don't sleep

Sucking a strawberry now, coming back from nightmare land. I met a friend there and he died, right in front of me after we climbed this huge mountain after we went swimming in some dark, snake-infested waters. After we looked at each others' eyes and heard each others' silence he fell and lay at my feet like a piece of burnt wood. But I talked to a man I met on that road and he said I could go on eBay to just do it; type in his name and add the details like, you know, the man said, lifting his Tyroler hat, you say you need the spare parts for your friend 'X' here. And he pointed at the piece of wood on the asphalt as if it was a type of *shtick* you could easily replace.

The feather on his hat danced in the wind when he waved goodbye and I stood alone again and cried because I needed a new heart for myself.

I sat on the road in the sun and looked left and right with a laptop heavy on my knees. I was naked. On the left the animals were dying and on the right, the children. What was I going to do when I ran out of battery?

Sucking on another strawberry, should I buy a Tyroler hat, categorize my friends to prevent them from dying? My hands are limp, I can't steer my vehicle in my sleep. I can't even listen to a man on a road who gives me Tyroler advice. *Nah fraulein fruhstuck?*

Solitude Snow White

At night the dwarf language appears
On my smallest screen, my precious phone
It lights up in the dark like a star
A beacon on my bedside table
It tells me that the dwarf has just left Snow White
And is having her apple for a midnight munch

His Snow White wouldn't score very high
On a general, wisdom, knowledge, beauty contest level
Whereas: I am the poisoned one
But my name is not Snow White
That's why I'm lying here: alone

That dwarf has taken to working at night
Hey, he says, Ho, he does
And not so much more is written on my screen
So: I am left to dream and dream
Of the beautiful dwarf
Roaming in some satellite space
His heart heavy with the swallowed cold stone
Of the badly-digested toxic fruit

I am the one with books bound
On my bedside table, a golden throat
And the ringing of diamond chimes as a gift
From my good fairies in my eager ears
I am the poisoned one

Yesterday I locked myself away
In a cubicle with the wretched witch
She told me to give her something,
Something that belonged to the dwarf
As far as I searched, on screens,
In my world, on my body: It was his,
All his.
So the spell was on me: Alone

The hours fill the night
And my small screen keeps flashing
Star after fallen star,
Sores for my sad eyes

The dwarf is taming a dragon
At work, important work, he says
But instead of flames I see ashes
And he's still there
At three-thirty, four, he is everywhere.

At five I lie in my coffin.

Belle

The light was yellow, ochre-cored
I was in the middle of it: Glowing.
I was the first phosphorescent being
It was nothing.
I was with you, I was Belle.

It was October and the Beast doesn't travel
During that month.
He's fastidious, he says
And the F sticks in between his uneven teeth
Like a straw, limp and empty,
With drool coming down his tongue,
Which I drink like dew.
I was with you, I was Belle.

I am homesick for the Beast
Having fish for breakfast
In Ventspils, Latvia.
The crusaders' dead knuckles
Tracing ice tracks on the windows
Reminding us with their nails
Dry, tick, tacking, like a tiny tickle
On a taut drum
That fish is fine for fighters.

The fish was staring at me
Its melted eye had a copper glow
As if it had been smoked in the sun, like that other beast.
My eye – his eye – met once
Under the sun and then the moon.
Before he swam he had devoured
Half my toes and all of my fingers.
He nearly convinced me too
That we'd both grow gills that way

And swim a common sea – get strong –
Stay, stay, stay, stay, he said
I couldn't move a muscle anymore,
I had to be another Belle and drink Baltic juice
In Ventspils, Latvia.

But for that glow
He would not have recognized me
When I came back, crippled
Starved by that hungry month of October.
Beast, beast, beast, beast, said I
Nothing is and nothing will be everything.
I am Belle.

A Rose with a Name

Ernest Hemingway shouted outside the Parisian dwelling of Gertrude Stein, "a rose was a rose, was an onion" because he was drunk and she had thrown him out, being the prim and proper American, after all. Stein, with her airs of *grande bohemienne* did not appreciate Hemingway's alliterations of her literary pose "a rose is a rose is a rose". A rose by any other name would smell as sweet. Would it really, Juliet? My dear Shakespearean heroine could have been crying fake tears here. If the rose had smelled like an onion.

Once, a good few years ago, I was asleep in a tall bed. A carved and painted statue of a Madonna was watching over me in the hot Spanish afternoon. The bells of a nearby church and the cooing doves had lulled me into the most secure of sleeps. I had abandoned my limbs to the sheet and drifted in my dreams. When I woke up I was aware of somebody looking at me from the foot of the bed. He called me "my onion" in a moment of tenderness when I had the feeling I had just woken up as a voluptuous rose. Tinted pink by the sun and sleep, I would have preferred a petalled reference to my appearance. Ah, vanity rules over love.

Why this memory on this Dublin evening when it is getting colder again. And darker. And all the voices speak to me of their blues on the phone, in the rooms. *It rains in my heart, comme il pleut sur la ville.*

I sing Debussy on a light, suspended breath. Actually, I would be quite happy right now to be called: An onion.

Jellyfish

And a good thing it was that I was stung by a French jellyfish. Why French, that's not fair; maybe it came drifting in from Spain or Greece. Its consistency and stinging tentacles did remind me of a person.

I got the picture, its firm and floaty body was decorated in attractive colours. As long as it swam in my eyesight and not beside me in my favoured waters it was faintly endearing in its blubbery charm, so small and yet with such a far reach to hurt. I felt the sting at night when I woke up for my three o'clock agony. I somehow suspected the jellyfish to be envious of other sea creatures for not being able to produce their own song like whales or dolphins. Stinging is their only way to communicate. Every night I soothed myself with a shapeless song, a bit of *Radiohead*, dead composers, sighs by myself to even out the streaks of the tentacles. Then, in my thoughts, I replanted the so-needed animals back in the sea, the ones that keep the jellyfish at bay.

Ah, pollution of our earth, of our minds. It looks like I surround myself with the right animals most of the time. They are all able to cry out: Watch out for the jellyfish

But then, at times, even I go deaf and suffer major stinging. *La reine est morte, vive la reine!!*

Short Poems

Les petits poèmes, short poems are like short skirts, flying in the summer wind, revealing a lot of body and even sometimes, *mais oui*, rarely, a little soul. One-liners can be just there, like the right man in the right place, or fall flat on their face and in the end mean, nothing. Nothing.

I have started playing at the Grand Casino again, my last game is down, my new game is up. *Rien ne va plus.*

Amsterdam

How do you remember a city
when yours is the flight of a bird?
In a white span of wings
you drew lines in the frozen light
describing somebody's dream
without noticing

while the houses stood empty and over-lit
along the grim winter mirror called *gracht*
you flew your fading shadow
– maybe catching the only ray of sunshine –
over the bridges and into somebody's dream
again without noticing

they had names for you
ground from a harsh alphabet
the bread was plentiful –
but the heart in the giving hands
was cold and needed to be fed – just like you –
fed with a dream that went unnoticed
while you flew out to sea

and you tasted the cracked salt
on your beak again
and you let your sharp eye
cleave the waves
in search of a silverfish.

Amsterdam Sunday

Goeiemorgen, zondag, Sunday, good day. I stand at my tall window, not yet dressed for the day, a child glued to my hip, Mozart, slow movement of the clarinet concerto filling the room with comfort for the ear and the heart. I look down at the water in the canal and at my neighbours struggling to get a wooden boat moving. The whole family is dressed in hats and cardigans and look like *auld* Dutchies from a Jan Steen painting. Gone are their ever trendy clothes and their VIP allures. A thick smoke comes from the motor cabin. The melody line of the clarinet soars through the room so strongly that I think it catches the sunlight and I briefly think of a contemporary of Mozart, Salieri, a powerless composer when it came to the Other's talent. Talent is a hard one to nurture and to honour. Look at them, down there, them there, having trouble to get their boat going. And they are so brilliant on a stage. We giggle, we *giechelen*, my daughter and I, hand in hand.

On Sunday, the canal is quiet until my mother's loud hairdryer, the sound her car makes, comes roaring down the cobblestones and the sun lights up her face, young and fresh in her old age. She hops up the stairs talking in her high voice, carrying books, goodies, stories. For us. She drinks strong coffee and let's the smoke from her cigarette drift with some literary comment or quotation she has just come up with, when I find something to complain about in life. I must go on, I can't go on. My child is now her grandchild, showing off her new skills on the harp while I sing a simple song to the accompaniment of her tiny fingers. Sunday knocks on the door with people coming in and out and all of us go for a stroll under the cold light in the sky which means the promise of frozen-over canals. Amsterdam sleeps since the 18th century. We live its well-oiled cultural life filled with the latest progress in art. The merchants continue rolling the coins around in a civilized manner. That was some time ago. Sundays are still Sundays, but there is a new fear in the veins of the *auld* Dutchies. Amsterdam *die stad op palen*. My Sunday is a Dublin one. My mother's voice sounds on in music and quotations, my child has detached herself from my hip.

Iranian Persian, My Darling

Leilisjan, pronounced with a soft *sjj* and a slightly curled up tongue, will hit the right Iranian as "darling." Three years ago I learned to sing that word accompanied by some musical arabesques played on the many strings of a "santour" by an old man with an older beard. He taught me Persian songs, for every three words of Farsi well pronounced I got a cookie or a savoury snack, sent to him by his family in Iran. He lived in Paris in a loft, with a lot of ladders; there was a very high one that led to an open loo. I climbed it once and lost my shoes on the way. He was not a very wise man, except when he started to play. At once I was wrapped up in transparent silks and transported into a thousand and one days of music. But that word "sweetheart", or "darling" or "beautiful one" *vous parlez Farsi? On me dit*, last night I sang it close to someone's ear and then they said it, that they had shed a tear when they heard me before. That was in a square in the open air and Omar Khayam himself (in spirit) had turned Dublin into a blazing hot city.

Bombs were exploding in London that day, like bombs are exploding in "X" now. Who, who, whhhhoow, prefers that, to the sweet sound of *Leilisjan*, my darling?

Song

I want to read you true poems at night
I want to make love to you
I want to wander through those years
That separate us
I want to make love to you
I want to listen to our music
I want to suffer it and
Laugh high notes with you
I want to feed you hope
When I tell you fairytales
Cruel and sunny
Dark and deep
I want to make love to you
I don't want to leave your nest
I don't want to go home
I want to make love to you
I want to brush your hair
And talk about some global affair
I want to take life to you
And season your time with white pepper
Lengthen your ears
Sweeten your juices
Ride the palest of your dreams
Listen to your pleasure-infested screams
I want to make love to you
I want to be the fruit in your mouth
And live off the salt of your earth
I want to be the sting in your existence
I want to bring you four seasons
I want to reduce my voice to your whisper
I want to be the song line
You hang on to for sheer survival
I want to make love to you

Chanson

Je veux te lire de vrais poèmes la nuit
Je veux te faire l'amour
Je veux m'évader à travers ces années
Qui nous séparent
Je veux te faire l'amour
Je veux écouter notre musique
Je veux la souffrir
Et rire des notes aigues avec toi
Je veux te nourir de l'espoir
Quand je te raconte des contes de fées
Cruels et ensoleillées
Sombres et profonds
Je veux te faire l'amour
Je ne veux pas quitter ton nid
Je ne veux pas rentrer chez moi
Je veux te faire l'amour
Je veux te brosser les cheveux
Et discuter le monde a deux
Je veux t'amener la vie
Et l'assaisoner de poivre blanc
Elonger tes oreilles
Sucrer tes flots
Monter le plus pale de tes rêves
Ecouter tes cris infestes de plaisir
Je veux te faire l'amour
Je veux être le fruit dans ta bouche
Et vivre du sel de ta terre
Je veux être la morsure de ton existence
Je veux t'amener quatre saisons
Je veux reduire ma voix à ton murmure
Je veux être la ligne de chant
À laquelle tu te suspens pour survivre
Je veux te faire l'amour

Cannot Write Songs

All night long I tried to write a song. I had the ingredients stirring in my head and my heart: loud and clear. But neither words nor music were anywhere near. I have poems singing to me and music sailing by, but I can't write a simple song. I have to strip off words and sounds and let my ears fly.

Heavy as a Butterfly

That is not the best of names for such an enchanting creature. *Schmetterling* is or *mariposa*. The colours are already there! It's so good to be able to enjoy some things in a different language. Last night, after the day in the streets carrying presents and meeting somebody who told me how to get my perfect acoustics around my voice forever, I wrapped a woman in my shawl. She was cold but we had to watch the city from a roof terrace and talk about the dead and the living and the in-between. Strangely enough the sky embraced us as if we were the oldest of friends. *On parlait papillon.* Then there were Italian, French, Portuguese, Swedish voices in between lots of food, and they all wanted my music. But I couldn't. I had been a heavy butterfly the night before, singing in a bathtub, with the violin stroking my ear, getting my wings up till too late, ignoring the painful left one, ignoring the darkness that was groping at me.

Come, fly, till the dust comes off and you lose your colours. I'm a moth now, too close to the first flame of light. Burn.

Haya! Heya! Kesckemet! A Tale Well Told

Alright: These are helpless expressions of overdoing it (sound wise) HEYA HAYA! because I have a stomach ache and have much work to do, although... *kesckemet*, that word only occurred in a Brahms song and now I find it at a Kletschmer festival. It all comes together today.

Yes, I was trying to remember a story told by a man to another man, I was sitting beside that man, if my memory serves me well, and it does most of the tam time, and the story was one of ghosts and witches in a small but beautiful land, and the man telling the story ate a steak dripping with blood while he talked and we stared: Petrified with fear and disbelief. For he had told us that a uniquely Irish created figure was actually a product of the imagination of a witch from his country. AHA. That was a long time ago. But time means nothing to those who want to get the truth out of a fairytale so I rang the man who had blood dripping down his chin back then and asked him to retell the tale. He was polite and official and important, because that is his job, and he said he never told a story like that. But then the other man who had sat beside me in our petrification rang, coincidentally, important as well, surrounded by his bodyguards and bloohaha he could still remember the tale of the witch from this non-Irish country that had created the tale of the bloody creature. I was not the one who turned my story into an untold one; the other man was the one who claimed his story was .... a-i-r and so: Am I the witch and is he the one who created the myth? How easy fairytales come to life in the lands of Nosferatu or Keschkemet.

Little Red Riding Hood

The children were conceived with Europe
Raised in different languages
Baptized in one: English
We sit together in a large car
Driving past the prosperous Latvian farms
I keep my hoodie up, up.
He hisses in his horny way:
"Your granny's bones are out there in the woods."
I recognize the Wolf straight away
He's there at the back of the car
And his coarse paws are on me
Pretending to teach me his name "*ielel*"
Which means nothing but wolf in Latvian.
He's checking out one of my nipples
Making sucky, sucky sounds
Of alcohol-fuelled saliva.

The woods are wonderful,
Full of mushrooms, our driver says
So we stop to go picking.
The husband, the children
All telling their mushroom memories to the trees
The fairytale runs from Bohemia to Teutonic Latvia
How mushrooms are thriving on porous grounds
Their stalks firmly planted in mystery.

Standing at a clearing – quietly
I can hear them through the thick blood red fabric of my hoodie:
The same children, the same as us,
Thirty thousand murdered and buried here in 1941
With filled baskets in hand, just like me.

Blood or "Le Sang des Autres"

The shots ricocheting against the flanks of the mountains so early in the morning that my sleepy subconscious has not even registered the chiming bells yet, yet......

We are in Sarajevo, suddenly. *Le jour de chasse est arrivé*, o glory, the Hunt, *la Casa*, funny how the same word for hunt in Spanish means matrimony and hunt, a coincidence? Oh. I am supposed to organize a concert programme for next season in the lovely Roman Church, surrounded by shady trees. I am supposed to eat a rabbit tonight and the man told me two days ago with a macho smile on his ancient face "*je vais le tuer*, I'm gonna kill it". Am I still hungry? For rabbit? Shall I suck the raw head raw? Oh. How sad his eyes were, the old boar, *sanglier*, in his stinky little hut. The man had caught him as a baby and wanted to fatten him up. He did and then he loved his fat boar and kept it as a pet. Speaking of matrimony: Do we like to fatten each other up and keep each other as sad pets? Oh. I talked to the traumatized wild animal, unbearable in his smell and even more in the way it looked at me, was I at least bringing it some food for solace? This morning they're shooting the furtive beasts that I saw yesterday on the path, running around with shifty movements, the eagle circling with its eyes on a snake I couldn't see, the stillness of the view and nature intact, the Pyrenees with wolves and bears, not far, the blue sea not far, humans were far, very far away, except for. Oh. Now I can imagine what it is like to hear shots in the morning and become completely unnerved by it, even though they are meant for the beasts, not me. What's the difference? In the afternoon I saw them hanging from the hooks in the *Salle des fêtes*, the hall of feasts. The blast of blood and wild odours was out in the streets, the dogs had blood on their teeth and in their fur, drenched, and the men had aprons, hiding their male satisfaction by rubbing long killer knives clean on their bellies.

I had to think of the concentration camps, I had to, who was hung on hooks again? Blood is blood and mine surged and I threw up under the Southern Sun with the taste of raw meat in my mouth. Oh.

A Point of View

Words, words, words, a handshake in the street. We all talk about the same thing yet what seems right to me seems wrong to another and even if I walk with Nietzsche beside good and evil I still want to keep my melodies pure, why can I not dwell in song alone and hide and find the corner of that umbrella back, a tiny corner, *petit paradis*, paradee, a feathered leafy tree.

All the Other Answers

I hold my breath because I can't hear it: The truth. If my heart stopped, if my pulse died down, if I became a ghost and moved into another body for these cherished seconds in which I could really hear. Why did Mahler long for Fortissimo when all I hear in his music is a hoarse whisper, the scratching of strings like vocal chords in an ever-blowing stark wind? I sat looking down at the river in Andalusia Argentina listening to its swelling while the Palomino horses were bathing in between the rocks like Centaurs. My mother had died weeks before and the earphones on my ears soothed me with Mahler's whispers, loud or soft; always a whisper. The only thing that was loud was my pain over her soul that had gone from the hard and cold body I had dressed up as my mother. It was morning then and when the evening came the river roared up during a thunderstorm and ripped trees and animals to pieces, floating then in the silent waters, ever silent, dead, death.

Walkabout

So far all is set in steel:
The yearning and the suffering
Cannot be bent.

We could go to Venice
Very early one morning
With the song of our night
Still in our heads, ringing desire
So loud the clanking of metal on metal
The lash of lust causing cold sparks to fly
Causing a far deeper pain than any hot branding:
Cold steel pressed on cold skin
Cannot leave a burning mark.

But, as I said
We should go to Venice
And when we travel I tell you
Sometime ago
One-two and more lovers
Came with me
The last one rearranged a drooping flower
In my hair.

We are travelling towards a glassblower's furnace
So early in the morning
That we can pretend it is still night

Or we could walk on
Through the Soukh in Istanbul
And pick up small, shining items
Like the particles of sound that
Emerge from my throat when I sing
Breakable butterflies
That you would like to catch

Hold their glow instead
It might warm in your hands
You will want to steal it from me
While we walk through the Soukh of Istanbul

Admiring all this subterranean gold.
This place has no windows
Only dark tunnels full of costly promises
But somehow I can see the sun rise

Einstein said that if the honeybee were extinct we (*wir menschen*) would not be able to live on earth anymore. The honeybee, apparently quickly on the way out, is of ultimate importance for our crops, no, no, *non, nein, nyet, nee* I do not want to continue.

Let's be romantic shall we and imagine we spend all that money used for trash, used for crushing people and crashing the world to recreate the little bodies and soft stinging of the honeybee. I don't want to spend the last four years of my life munching grain and forget the colour of fresh growing green. I want to walk in the mountains and hear you buzzing around lavender and thyme, honeybee. I want to lie in the grass with you hovering around me. Can't do the sweet thing, the words don't work; want to taste the honey. How ironic that I was walking the coastline and the lukewarm seawater up to our thighs with a German scientist yesterday while he was gesticulating wildly in his enthusiasm to explain his neutron theories, nuclear energies. We went back to the Curies, because I'm ignorant, especially when it comes to physics, and I need to know stuff right from the beginning. We walked and talked about Einstein, and a bit of music, and then into a wide horizon because he said he just did all that research for the research – *an sich* – we barely noticed switching from English to German and back because I wanted to know more and more, what the goal was. What would happen in the end with his work, what was he using his clever head for? It was warm, the boats posed in perfect harmony on the sea, and all the time there was a stinging and longing in me, did I miss something, somebody? The bee? Oh honey!

A Cold Poem
for my father: Maurits Mok

You lifted me up:
It was not high enough

For me to reach my father's poem
And see the mountain road
Where he hugged me after a month of summer camp
And pre-teenage intrigues.

I showed my father the river where I caught my trout
And let it go in its silver and slime
I showed him the tree where the eagle perched
The tents and tables
The wild artichoke growing underneath my hard crib
Raw and edible
A place in the sky where lightning struck
Every evening
And the grass circle where we whispered and danced
As I danced towards him
When I was his child full of his poetry
But when I saw him on that mountain road
With his red 2cv behind him
Shining in the stark Provençal sun
He was my father who lifted me up in his arms

It was not high enough:
For the fish to be a trophy of liberty
The artichoke a triumph of discovery
For me to be dancing Judith again
Like in that line of my father's poetry

Could I have shared the admiration for Napoleon that Heinrich Heine and Stendhal had? Their emotional abandon when it came to admire Napoleon led them to write great poems and even follow the Great Soldier around as far as Russia.

Much as I like to *schlepp* these great writers' books around the globe with me and live in admiration for their (un)wise words on the page, they live on in my mind and a bit in my heart too I'd say, but admiration for a public figure?

I've never done it.

I sat in bed yesterday resting my voice for an exciting singing gig tomorrow, rereading Tolstoy's nearly sensual descriptions of the Russians battles against Napoleon in *War and Peace*. Don't think anybody has ever surpassed his magnificent descriptions of these grim battles. What do I know anyway?

I can only admire the poor sod who followed Napoleon sitting comfortably on his horse Marengo to Russia in the big snows, while leaving his heart behind, kept in a jar in a cupboard in Venice by his web-footed mistress. The soldier survives and goes back to Venice to have loads of web footed kiddies with the mistress. What's all that got to do with admiration? Heine, Stendhal, the miserable soldier and many others poured their full hearts' contents into the admiration they felt for the rider of Marengo.

See that's how I visualize him, a small man on a great horse posing as the king of the world, definitely the world's biggest chancer at the time. I'm taking my Tricorne off for him, just to slam it even harder back on my head again: I need shelter from the rain and the wind in this country. But what about my lack of heart for the matters of admiration?

Have I been riding my imagined Horse for all these years, without an army to follow me or a couple of countries to rule? No, I don't want to rule either. Except on stage where I will sing my heart out until it's empty and ready to be fuelled with the love and admiration of my public. Five minutes MS MOK….

France

Being with them this afternoon made me want to leave this country even more. Travel, not for work purposes the way I usually do but for leisure. I had a trip planned involving sea and sun but now, while I was telling loved-ones about our trips to France, I wanted to go back there. How often did I drive up the hill from Taulignan to *les corps neuf* in the late afternoon *entre chien et loup*, between dog and wolf as they say, and greeted the mountains and the wide open view with a smile, singing. Then down through the vineyards and apricot trees towards the farm with its turret from the thirteenth century. The children naked in the river, a couple of writers and artists friends dealing with the *aperitif*, the *saucisson* in slices on the board, strong mustard, *caviar d'aubergine* and wit, sometimes poems, on the tip of their tongues. My skin warm from the sun, hardly any clothes on, my feet bare and free, I like to drive barefoot. But that's not what I told them about this afternoon; it was about the driving down from Holland to Menton with my sister and my parents. I would be accused of acute *snobisme* if I mentioned my sister and I singing parts of *The Magic Flute* at the back of our Citroen 2cv. First we had a grey one then it turned red. Yes, we were small and we sang Mozart for fun until my father had had enough and we stopped along the road so he could smoke a cigar. Then, at lunchtime, we drove around looking for his perfect spot to have our picnic. The tarpaulin was spread on the grass the napkins were out, cheeses and patés and fresh baguettes on plates and boards, butter in a glass and aluminum container, glasses for milk and juice. We had time, lots of time apparently. Towards five o'clock we would look for a rural hotel, eat a large rural dinner and we would stroll around the village and join the local kids watching the train come in and then leave the station again; the event of the day. We drove for four days while the mountains grew higher at the horizon and then around us, and our final hotel before our destination would serve *Muscat*. My parents were merry, sang and drank, and I slept by an open window, breathing in the smells of the Provence, my favoured smells. Thyme and lavender. That's what it still smells like in my favoured dreams of travel.

Make or Break

They are standing in a Dublin vegetable shop;
Castanea Dentata, chestnuts said she,
Fauchon, remembering Paris, *Marrons Glacés*:
The faded butterfly wings of the wrapping paper
The box, half-open, like a promising, sweet smile
Her fingers reaching out for what her tongue would like: Love.

We Irish, said he, play Conkers.

The Wizard's Walk

What he said he saw in my eyes
was mostly the source for his beginning.
Merlin of miracles waded in water
going up the crowded midnight streets.
My hand in his, me counting the
times I recognized this:
There had been so many nights
when I hoped he would lead me to the water
because every time I saw myself reflected in it
a pulse, a push, a wave in my blood
would make me more eager to sail with him
on the indigo, no cobalt, maybe that Prussian blue sea.
What he said he saw in my eyes
was nothing but his longing for a future full of childhood memories.
And for that I wanted him, this Merlin of Miracles.
Later that night had lost its colour
as all we walked through was washed out.
Some sepia-tinted creatures
stood, soaked, incarnating a vague contour of a Caravaggio or Bosch,
begging on the corners we knew to ignore.
Though, in my thoughts, he still held onto my hand
he walked, in fact, ahead of me
and guided me with that certain, boyish aplomb, through hell,
back and shoulders slightly slumped, snakes sculpted in his hair.
What he saw in my eyes he said
was something I remembered he told me:
that he would be this Merlin of Miracles.
And for that I loved him.
I thought he just loved the idea of my eyes, of me
some feeling fired up by the wind flying over
the water in the Liffey
that lead mirror in which I observed his features,
Some feeling that would die down in the early morning light
when he stood smoking on the bridge, blowing a cloud in my mouth

so we could both inhale as if we were one.
We didn't speak you see
Where earlier on they had danced, wrapped rhythmically around our legs
and their fabric was flung to a sound as strong as a storm,
the bottom of our trousers now equally dragged down
by a dead weight of wet and dirt
as I followed my Merlin of Miracles.
I was with him; I continued to walk through hell
until we reached the edge and he, finally, placed his fingers on my face
and turned it, gently, far enough to show me his well.

Hands in Cages Louise Bourgeois

Wringing of the hands in enclosed spaces; bedroom, bathroom, workroom, rooms of her life reconstructed, when I wander up the spinning, Frank Lloyd Wright built, Guggenheim gallery, up, up as if in a dream to look at the inner life of a woman. Louise Bourgeois, old now and ageless for ever. I bow to the early graceful totems of her early years; they are like solidified sighs, breathing upwards, decorated with a great sense of humor, laughing at herself even. Good. I like to do that too. A lot. I know for a fact that I like to play along with Louise and anything she is dishing out in front of my eyes; a wave of sculpted phalluses, veiled in soft white alabaster coming at her in her sixties? Memories of her mother as a giant spider, hairy, dressed in precious cloth? Memories of my own, immediately. But I see them together, mother and father, a parent beast. I do not sculpt or draw, I sing I write. It was so hot, my last days in NY. My feet walked, my mouth talked, my eye was bloodshot, very badly. I woke up with it. And without a Muse. A cloud of blood covered the blue in my eye. So everyone looked at it twice when they were talking to me. A lot of people were talking to me because I sang in the street with a jazz band, and I wore polka dots on my dress. Back to Louise, and me in the tiny NY bathroom, wringing my hands for a moment in powerless pain because of a very recent memory, possibly a dream I had, that coloured my eye red. I don't draw, I write and I sing.

Beethoven in New York
Für Elise

This night is on me like a blank sheet.
I have to write
Of people playing music that
Fills the subway with my submerged sounds,
As if I am a whale vibrating through the thick of times,
Communicating that my name is: Beethoven,
A man of music in a storm of voices,
A choir, an army of American instruments,
People playing my music, people judging me,
How I rode this crushing wave of emotions.

I wake to chaos and constellations in my head,
Thinking: I will have to tell her
I heard this choir supporting some statement about me,
Thinking: it's one breath of mine against three of hers,
That's what our rhythm seems to be.

I hear this couple talking,
Two voices modulating into one,
Softly speaking spectres of promise.

I spy on her asleep
Sensing a child in her with too many dreams
To choose from, her jaws clenched
To keep them inside till they rot
While she dies slowly in her sleep.

Casual chords coming from open car windows
Signalling to me that these are New York symphonies
And also: That Elise is still here, with me,
That I must write for her.

Her eyes closed in the half-light
A film of cold sweat on her pale skin
Her neck exposed to my murderous mind
And me slicing through her sighs
While all I feel is music, my music melting
In the smothering air we breathe, one against three.

She came to me. Her mouth
Full of crunched-up words
A meaningless alphabet to her tune
She turns her slender body away

So I can wipe it dry and write,
Write on her bony back, as on a blackboard,
Feeling the whipping flame on my eyes
When I see too much of her
And want to write, my love, my love,
But instead I write two notes – *ta – ta*
A diminished second, and from there: oOn.

This I will hear until I go deaf
And then it will last.

Two notes dancing in a ripped-up dawn
I, sadly, take to my formal clothes, a composer again,
My mind still playing with the thought of her body
Gasping – *ta – ta* – while I brush my hair,
Reacquire my intense stare.
Her glow on me in the mirror,

It is her planet I live on,
Nothing belongs to me but music.

I bring broken notebooks.
Winging my way down to the New York subway,
My history in my shaking hands.

The entrance is like a gargoyle upside-down.
I dive into its steam-spouting mouth,
My pores oozing fear
I walked this score
I see, I can hear
The mini-masters who play my music have sorted me out
While they keep talking about Elise and me
Hammering out her tune – *ta – ta*.

I am inside the whale, in my ears, in my heart
Wanting to fight against the pulse – *ta – ta*.
But it's here, played on a steel drum
Beet – Beethoven on a pot, a drum looking like
A caved-in reproduction of our gutted earth,
A rivulet of my music, my feelings scored.
This tender tone: For Elise.
Ta – ta – ta – ta – ta from there: Onwards.
And they say I have Asperger Syndrome.

Skull: Mine circles: My neck is caught. I take a train

Over the weekend I visited a cemetery. Not enough trees, old graves reminiscent of my old friends the graves of the princes Troubetzkoy in Menton where I liked to sit as a nine/ten year old in the *cimetière* and salute: *les fourgons*. I had many dreams and little sleep in the last nights because trains kept running in and out of the stations of my subconscious. And I kept going back to take the one that took me to a beloved one. Last night I arrived somewhere and was told that I needed to enter some circles, but the circles were hard and around my neck and I could hardly breathe when a voice said 'you are here already' Golgotha! My skull had arrived? Golgotha means path of skulls in Aramaic. Golgotha means nothing to me but the words sung in the Passions by Johan Sebastian Bach. The days that I sang for the first time in the Matthew Passion and we sang the haunting words of a fanatical crowd, *wohin*: where to? And the answer would be firm; *nach Golgotha*. To Golgotha. I was seventeen and overcome by Bach's musicality and humanity. I was in Scheveningen, Holland and walked on the beach with a boy after the performance. My skull is younger than that; it has only started to travel in musical circles apparently.

Baudelaire and the blue moonstone

...from us where the clear blue is all love and happiness. Twice this week I walked with the poet Baudelaire. First I told him how surprised I was that he had said something about my ex-dancer's legs, because I thought men like him wouldn't even notice me, let alone speak of my legs. Then we walked through Paris, the Parc du Luxembourg on a bright day and a brighter night, his talking was a maze of words, he was high on the *poème de hashish* and my talk was of the blue moonstone that I need to acquire as a third eye. But eyes are a gift. I have been given two blue eyes, and now a third one is watching me. Waiting to give me an even more blurred vision of my world. Baudelaire and I watched the rot of it, my world, sniffed the roses in the park, smelled the stink of those who walked by, eyes closed, in the company of splendid rags. We sat on the floor of his autumn palace and he held my leg in his hand, until his eyes had polished it into a smooth memory and I told him nothing more but...*de nous le bleu clair n'est qu'amour et bonheur*...Nothing more...

Adio Querido
for Shane Booth

Upside down in your
Bright blue painted *currach*
You prevent me from drowning
By throwing me some lifeline: A song of love
But then, you watch me: How I slowly sing and sink.
Coldly, a smile folded in your dry cheeks
You hold me like a wrench in your mindless hands,
So you can pump fresh blood
Into my voice, that bulges and bursts
And floods the music that fails to make your heart beat
Or your body sail.

A flicker of hope is the flash of the knife
Coming out of the night's dark waters
I think: Where are all these hooded people going
Wound-up puppets, the invisible push
Of time in their backs.
I am sitting out the hours not knowing
why I am still afloat with the memory of your *currach*
and that once I get hold of the knife
I can cut my chords,
Lose the lifeline,
Suffer the sharpness of silence
Listen to death: Singing about the Irish Messiah.

Choices Incarnate

If I was to enter an order today, a brother/sisterhood, and I had to choose the persona of an animal what would I be?

Late, late, last night I went down to the water. The swans were crying for food. Loudly, screeching. I gathered bread from the cupboard and stuffed large chunks of dried-out cake and bread in their beaks. When a swan lifts up its neck it can be as tall as you. I was intimidated by their presence and the poverty of the food I had on offer. A young one followed me around, pulling at my clothes.

Yeats said: *swans are the reflection of the human soul.* There was another large bird hiding out in the dark: A cormorant. My cormorant, the only one on the canal.

She is always there trying to fly with the swans, I even saw her courting a swan, spreading her large black wings to impress the fairy-white creature opposite her.

For a split second the swan flashed its wings back at her and then hid his head.

Recently people talked about incarnation around me, what would I be, indeed what animal would I be? No time to think, I said: I would be an eagle with the voice of a nightingale. But the thing is: I have been associating with the cormorant, convinced that I am she, she is me. *Cor mo rant,* raven of the sea, pelicans, protectors, symbols of Sephardim.

I prefer tasting the salt and the sweet - water - and be able to fish for the food of my choice. I prefer to be black-feathered and have the courage to court a white feathered one.

Could I be a cormorant?

Never a swan!

JUDITH MOK was born in Bergen in the Netherlands. She has published three novels and three books of poetry as well as short stories. *Gods of Babel* is her first collection of poetry in English. Her short stories have been short-listed twice for the Francis MacManus award and her first novel, *The Innocents at the Circus,* for the Prix de l'Academie Française. Her work has appeared nationally and internationally in literary magazines and anthologies. She has also written for radio and newspapers. Judith Mok travels the world as a classical singer.